Solitude
&
Contemplation

Look for these topics in the Everyday Matters Bible Studies for Women

Acceptance

Bible Study & Meditation

Celebration

Community

Confession

Contemplation

Faith

Fasting

Forgiveness

Gratitude

Hospitality

Justice

Mentoring

Outreach

Prayer

Reconciliation

Sabbath Rest

Service

Silence

Simplicity

Solitude

Stewardship

Submission

Worship

Solitude & Contemplation

Spiritual Practices
FOR EVERYDAY LIFE

HENDRICKSON PUBLISHERS

**Everyday Matters Bible Studies for Women—
Solitude & Contemplation**

© 2015 Hendrickson Publishers Marketing, LLC
P. O. Box 3473
Peabody, Massachusetts 01961–3473

ISBN 978–1-61970–630–9

Bible study written by Patricia Anders

Printed in the United States of America

First Printing—September 2015

Contents

Contemplation

Holy Habits

Spiritual Practices for Everyday Life

Everyday life today is busier and more distracting than it has ever been before. While cell phones and texting make it easier to keep track of children and each other, they also make it harder to get away from the demands that overwhelm us. Time, it seems, is a shrinking commodity. But God, the Creator of time, has given us the keys to leading a life that may be challenging but not overwhelming. In fact, he offers us tools to do what seems impossible and come away refreshed and renewed. These tools are called spiritual practices, or spiritual disciplines.

Spiritual practices are holy habits. They are rooted in God's word, and they go back to creation itself. God has hardwired us to thrive when we obey him, even when it seems like his instructions defy our "common sense." When we engage in the holy habits that God has ordained, time takes on a new dimension. What seems impossible is actually easy; it's easy because we are tapping into God's resources.

The holy habits that we call spiritual practices are all geared to position us in a place where we can allow the Holy Spirit to work in us and through us, to grant us power and strength to do the things we can't do on our own. They take us to a place where we can become intimate with God.

While holy habits and everyday life may sound like opposites, they really aren't.

As you learn to incorporate spiritual practices into your life, you'll find that everyday life is easier. At the same time, you will draw closer to God and come to a place where you can luxuriate in his rich blessings. Here is a simple example. Elizabeth Collings hated running household errands. Picking up dry cleaning, doing the grocery shopping, and chauffeuring her kids felt like a never-ending litany of menial chores. One day she had a simple realization that changed her life. That day she began to use her "chore time" as a time of prayer and fellowship with God.

Whenever Elizabeth walked the aisle of the supermarket, she prayed for each person who would eat the item of food she selected. On her way to pick up her children, she would lay their lives out before God, asking him to be there for them even when she couldn't. Each errand became an opportunity for fellowship with God. The chore that had been so tedious became a precious part of her routine that she cherished.

The purpose of these study guides is to help you use spiritual practices to make your own life richer, fuller, and deeper. The series includes twenty-four spiritual practices that are the building blocks of Christian spiritual formation. Each practice is a holy habit that has been modeled for us in the Bible. The practices are acceptance, Bible study and meditation, celebration, community, confession, contemplation, faith, fasting, forgiveness, gratitude, hospitality, justice, mentoring, outreach, prayer, reconciliation, Sabbath rest, service, silence, simplicity, solitude, stewardship, submission, and worship.

As you move through the practices that you select, remember Christ's promise in Matthew 11:28–30:

> *Come to me, all of you who are weary and carry heavy burdens. Take my yoke upon you. Let me teach you, because I am humble and gentle at heart, and you will find rest for your souls. For my yoke is easy to bear, and the burden I give you is light.*

Introduction

to the Practice of Solitude & Contemplation

I have discovered that all the unhappiness of
[people] arises from one single fact, that they
are unable to stay quietly in their own room.

BLAISE PASCAL

"People Prefer Electric Shocks to Being Alone with Their
Thoughts." Yes, according to a university study, it's true. In a
recent *Atlantic* article, writer Matthew Hutson reports that
Timothy Wilson of the University of Virginia conducted
eleven experiments. In most of the experiments, the par-
ticipants were asked to do nothing but sit alone with their
own thoughts for six to fifteen minutes. Apparently, many
of them—too many of them—had a difficult time doing this.
According to Hutson, "Subjects were wired up and given
the chance to shock themselves during the thinking period
if they desired." They had all experienced the unpleasant
electrical shock earlier, so they knew it was actually quite
painful. Hutson writes:

And yet, even among those who said they would pay money not to feel the shock again, a quarter of the women and two thirds of the men gave themselves a zap when left with their own thoughts. (One outlier pressed the button 190 times in the 15 minutes.) Commenting on the sudden appeal of electricity coursing through one's body, Wilson said, "I'm still puzzled by that."

In seeking a solution to this inability to sit alone for even fifteen minutes, Wilson's team "did find a small correlation between meditation experience and ability to entertain oneself, and they suggest that control over one's thoughts may be one appeal of meditation." There is hope for us yet!

Meditation can be defined as engaging in contemplation or reflection, focusing one's thoughts, reflecting, pondering. We can also call this "prayer." So it seems a logical conclusion that to train our thoughts to focus at all, we need to *practice* doing so, disciplining ourselves *spiritually*. We start by desiring to grow deeper in our relationship with God. But something different happens here in that it is *God* who must draw us and speak to us. Our part in this is that we need to stop what we're doing from time to time to be quiet enough to *listen* to that still, small voice.

Many people have the wrong idea about solitude and contemplation. They think they have to go off to a retreat center or camp in the middle of the woods (or build a small cabin by Walden Pond, if you happen to be Henry David Thoreau). While there's nothing wrong with this, most of us don't have time (or inclination or money) to indulge in this "ideal" setting. Our lives are too busy and we barely have time to catch our breath as it is. This, however, becomes a problem when we become too busy even for God, when the noise of our lives shuts out his gentle whisper or light knocking at the door.

But what does "solitude" really mean? In *Celebration of Discipline*, Richard Foster writes that "solitude is more a state of mind and heart than it is a place." You may be at your desk or in the kitchen—in the midst of a chaotic or highly stressful moment—when you find you need to stop what you're doing, take a couple of deep breaths, and refocus your mind and heart on God. Even one minute of calmly reorienting yourself can make a difference. And every once in a while, it's healthy—spiritually, mentally, and physically—to take off an afternoon or morning (or longer if possible) to spend time in solitude. As Virginia Woolf says, "To advance, one must retreat."

But are we *really* alone when we seek this solitude, are we *really* off by ourselves somewhere? In "Solitude for Extroverts" (*Everyday Matters Bible for Women*), Caryn Rivadeneira writes:

> The goal of solitude is not to be alone. The goal is to be with God. A triune God at that! A God who is a community within himself. Solitude is you, the Father, the Son, and the Holy Spirit. While we may be retreating from other humans, we're turning toward the miraculous three-in-one fellowship of the triune God.

Theologians call this *perichoresis*, which is a Greek word describing the relationship of the three persons of the Trinity—a community of being in a joyful "dance" as one God. *This* is the fellowship we are invited into!

Silence also plays a large role in the spiritual practice of solitude. Even when we're among others, we should be quick to listen and slow to speak. In this way, we can actually hear the other person, hear perhaps what God may be saying to us in that moment, and consider what we have heard and how we should respond (if at all). "God is in heaven, and you are here on earth. So let your words be few" (Ecclesiastes 5:2).

Contemplation is a discipline that is a bit harder to grasp. Deeper than meditation or prayer, it is more a lifelong process of sanctification. But what does this look like? Although there are many examples in Scripture of people who sought after God in this most earnest way, the story of Martha and Mary (Luke 10:38–41) shows us the obvious difference between an "active" and a "contemplative" (as defined by the anonymous fourteenth-century English monk in *The Cloud of Unknowing*).

While Jesus was visiting their home in Bethany, Martha rightfully busied herself with the practice of hospitality ("Martha welcomed him into her home"), while Mary "sat at the Lord's feet, listening to what he taught." Flustered by this, Martha complained to Jesus: "Lord, doesn't it seem unfair to you that my sister just sits here while I do all the work? Tell her to come and help me." Luke records Jesus' response: "My dear Martha, you are worried and upset over all these details! There is only one thing worth being concerned about. Mary has discovered it, and it will not be taken away from her."

In Mary we see what it truly means to practice contemplation and solitude—sitting at the Lord's feet and listening to what he has to teach us. But, like Martha, we need to keep in mind that while we are busy with our daily tasks, we are always in the Lord's presence. May this Bible study draw you closer to God as you earnestly seek after him. As James 4:8 says: "Come close to God, and God will come close to you."

Solitude

CHAPTER 1

"I Am Who I Am"

Meeting God in the Wilderness

So he got up and ate and drank, and the food gave
him enough strength to travel forty days and forty
nights to Mount Sinai, the mountain of God. There
he came to a cave, where he spent the night.

1 KINGS 19:8

*For this week's study, read Exodus 2–3,
1 Kings 19, and Matthew 17:1–13.*

Mount Sinai—the "mountain of God"—is a 7,500-foot
mountain situated at the southern end of the austere Sinai
Peninsula in Egypt. It is the place of the famous encounter
between the exiled Moses and God in the burning bush,
the birthplace of the Mosaic Law and the Ten Commandments, and a refuge for the weary prophet Elijah. In the
early years of the church, sometime in the sixth century,
monastic anchorites made the pilgrimage to the foot of this
holy mountain, establishing the Sacred Monastery of the
God-Trodden Mount Sinai—known today as St. Catherine's
Monastery, still a sanctuary for those willing to make the
arduous journey.

Although we don't know why God called Moses and Elijah to this particular mountain, we do know that he called them. As far as Moses could tell, he would be an Egyptian all his life. Drawn from the Nile, raised by Pharaoh's daughter, he lived in the lap of luxury among the pagan gods of Egypt. But the one true God—the God of Abraham, Isaac, and Jacob—had another plan for him.

After a foiled attempt to help his people (by killing an Egyptian who had been beating a fellow Hebrew), the Scriptures tell us that Moses was afraid Pharaoh would try to kill him (which proved true), and so he "fled from Pharaoh and went to live in the land of Midian" (Exodus 2:15). When he tried to help his people through his own strength, their reaction was harsh: "Who appointed you to be our prince and judge?" (Exodus 2:14). Who indeed.

After running away from Pharaoh's palace and journeying across the desert, Moses settled in Midian, married Jethro's daughter Zipporah, and fathered two sons. Years passed and we can only speculate how often—if at all—his thoughts swept back over the desert to where his people suffered in cruel slavery in Egypt. Then one day while out tending Jethro's flocks, Moses led the flock "far into the wilderness" (Exodus 3:3). He came to Mount Sinai and the rest is history: God spoke to him out of a burning bush, appointing him to free the Hebrew slaves, gathering them into a people for God. When Moses asked who he should tell the Hebrews had sent him, God answered, "I Am Who I Am. Say this to the people of Israel: I Am has sent me to you" (Exodus 3:14). After a devastating non-contest between Pharaoh and the Creator of the universe, the people journeyed from

Egypt, across the desert, to Mount Sinai—back to the wilderness where God had first spoken to Moses.

Despite the multitude of the twelve tribes of Israel that were now Moses' responsibility, God called Moses to solitude—to a very personal time with him on the holy mountain. There were two rounds of forty days and forty nights when Moses waited upon the Lord, hearing his instructions for the people, receiving the law and the Ten Commandments. It was a time of fasting and revelation, a time of speaking with God "face to face," but also of hiding from that face (the glory of which Moses' own face reflected after this special encounter). Although Moses was indeed special, the fact remains that it was *God* who called him on all occasions, God who spoke, and Moses who listened, enveloped in a cloud of glory.

In the time of King Ahab, the prophet Elijah was also called to this mountain in the Sinai Peninsula. After God's astounding defeat of the prophets of Baal and Elijah's order for their execution, Elijah had to run for his life from the murderous Jezebel—fleeing from the queen just as Moses had fled from Pharaoh. After traveling forty days and forty nights to Mount Sinai, he found shelter in a cave, coming to the end of his journey.

Then he heard God say, "Go out and stand before me on the mountain" (1 Kings 19:11). There was a "mighty windstorm" and then an earthquake and fire, but God was not in any of these violent manifestations of power. It was when Elijah heard "a gentle whisper" (1 Kings 19:12) that he knew he heard God's voice. He wrapped his face in his cloak and stepped outside the cave to listen. During a difficult period in Israel's history, Elijah had served the Lord well. But now he was tired and ready to hang up his prophet's mantel. God did not disagree and appointed Elisha as Elijah's replacement.

Centuries later, in the event known as the "Transfiguration," it was *Jesus* who met and talked with both Moses and Elijah (Mark 9:2–13). Peter, James, and John were astounded at this encounter, and Peter rambled on about building "shelters" as "memorials" (Mark says that Peter "didn't really know what else to say, for they were all terrified"!). Matthew 17:2–8 describes the account with a bit more drama:

> *As the men watched, Jesus' appearance was transformed so that his face shone like the sun, and his clothes became as white as light. Suddenly, Moses and Elijah appeared and began talking with Jesus. . . . A bright cloud overshadowed them, and a voice from the cloud said, "This is my dearly loved Son, who brings me great joy. Listen to him." The disciples were terrified and fell face down on the ground. Then Jesus came over and touched them. "Get up," he said. "Don't be afraid." And when they looked up, Moses and Elijah were gone, and they saw only Jesus.*

Jesus, the long-awaited Messiah, called out to the people of his day to listen to *his* voice, to what the Father had taught him (John 8:28). When challenged by the people, he told them that their father Abraham "rejoiced as he looked forward to my coming. He saw it and was glad" (John 8:56). When they responded that he wasn't old enough to have seen Abraham, he answered them with one of the most thrilling lines in all of literature: "I tell you the truth, before Abraham was even born, I Am!" (John 8:58).

Jesus—the great "I Am"—is the one who calls us today to listen to *his* voice. Notice how many times in the Gospel accounts Jesus says, "You have heard that it is said . . . But *I* say to you . . ." The law and the prophets had their role, but now it is God incarnate who speaks directly to us. Whenever the disciples recognized this, they were overwhelmed, sometimes even terrified. But to them—and to us—he says, "Don't be afraid."

Although we don't need to journey over the harsh Egyptian desert to meet God at Mount Sinai, God still calls us to meet with him. God desires those who worship him in spirit and in truth. He no longer dwells in the temple in Jerusalem, his glory filling the Holy of Holies. *Jesus* is the way, the truth, and the life. He is the great high priest and the lover of our souls.

Yahweh dwelled in a dark cloud over Mount Sinai and thundered when he spoke. Like the Israelites, we too may feel he is unapproachable—too holy for us to draw near him. There is a darkness that still seems to linger in our minds as we reach out toward him, desperate to know him, to be intimate with him. Mark Galli writes in "Listening for the Whisper" (*Everyday Matters Bible for Women*):

> *When you try to practice Elijah-like spirituality, says the author of* The Cloud of Unknowing, *you will at first feel a "darkness about your mind, or as it were a cloud of unknowing. You will seem to know nothing and feel nothing except a naked intent toward God in the depths of your being. Try as you might, this darkness, and this cloud will remain between you and your God. You will feel frustrated, for your mind will be unable to grasp him, and your heart will not relish the delight of his love." . . . But eventually, says this author, if "you hope to feel and see God as he is in himself, it must be within this darkness and this cloud."*

Regularly retiring to the dark cave, to the fearful quiet of silent prayer and meditation, to listen to the whisper is the first step in breaking free. . . . The darkness of mystery and silence opens up whole new vistas for us and gives us the ears to hear the whisper.

Jesus is the light that was to come into the world: "The light shines in the darkness, and the darkness can never extinguish it" (John 1:5). He is our light—yesterday, today, and forever.

For the law was given through Moses, but God's unfailing love and faithfulness came through Jesus Christ. No one has ever seen God. But the unique One, who is himself God, is near to the Father's heart. He has revealed God to us. (John 1:17–18)

God calls us to solitude, to time spent with him, listening to him, allowing him—as St. Francis of Assisi prayed—to enlighten the darkness of our hearts.

Jesus, lover of my soul,
Let me to Thy bosom fly,
While the nearer waters roll,
While the tempest still is high.
Hide me, O my Savior, hide,
Till the storm of life is past;
Safe into the haven guide;
Oh, receive my soul at last.
—Charles Wesley

As you study this chapter, think about what might be keeping you from truly approaching God and why.

1. Like Elijah, are you hiding in a cave—worn out and unsure what to do next? If so, what are you running from? Have you quieted yourself enough to hear what God might be saying to you in this situation?

2. In *Invitation to Solitude and Silence*, Ruth Haley Barton says that the natural chaos outside Elijah's cave can be viewed as a "metaphor for the inner chaos that surges within us when we stay in the presence of the Unchanging Real long enough for pretense and performance and *every other thing that has bolstered our sense of self* to fall away. When we have been stripped of external distraction, we face the fact that the deepest level of chaos is inside us, at our very core." What inner chaos rages within you?

3. Read Luke 4:1–13 about Jesus' testing in the wilderness for *forty days* and *forty nights*—which is also the amount of time spent by Moses and Elijah in their various encounters with God. Think about other times *forty* is mentioned in the Bible (for examples, see Genesis 7:4; Numbers 13:25; 14:33–34; 1 Samuel 17:16; Acts 1:3). What do you think is the significance of this number?

4. The desert has been viewed historically as an uninhabitable place. In fact, in Scripture we see great spiritual struggles (or punishment) taking place in the desert (or wilderness). In *Thoughts in Solitude*, Thomas Merton writes, "The desert used to be a place that no man wanted, and now everywhere is a desert." In a modern context, what do you think he means by that?

5. Merton writes, "Do not flee to solitude from community. Find God first in the community, then He will lead you to solitude." How can you find God in your community?

6. Notice in the Gospels how many times Jesus seeks out solitude, sometimes alone with the Father, other times with the disciples or a select few. But it was never long before he was back in the thick of his ministry. Read Matthew 17:14–20 and write down your thoughts, especially in light of the Transfiguration that had just happened up on the mountain.

You have not come to a physical mountain, to a place of flaming fire, darkness, gloom, and whirlwind, as the Israelites did at Mount Sinai. . . . No, you have come to Mount Zion, to the city of the living God, the heavenly Jerusalem, and to countless thousands of angels in a joyful gathering. (Hebrews 12:18, 22)

Points to Ponder

In *New Seeds of Contemplation,* Thomas Merton writes, "Our idea of God tells us more about ourselves than about Him." Depending on our relationships with our own fathers, sometimes we see God in the same way. How do you see God?

- As a loving father, someone you're close to?

- As a domineering and scary father, someone you want to avoid?

- As an overly busy father, someone you don't think has time for you?

- As an uninvolved father, someone you think doesn't care about you?

- As someone you never knew but always wanted to?

Prayer

As St. Francis of Assisi prayed:

Most High, glorious God,
enlighten the darkness of my heart and give me
true faith, certain hope, and perfect charity,
sense and knowledge, Lord, that I may carry out
Your holy and true command.

Add your prayer in your own words.

Amen.

Put It into Practice

"Although God had performed many miracles in the wilderness, [Israel] refused to trust him. I realized my own complaints weren't only negative words, they were grumblings against God. He's much bigger than any problem I face, and in his strength I can overcome anything. When I complain, it lets God know that I don't trust him. As with the manna and quail, I was graciously given the necessities in life. . . . So I decided to give up complaining."

—Linda Manes, "Complain, Complain," *Everyday Matters Bible for Women*

Let us not be like unbelieving Israel but reach out to God with childlike faith, trusting always in our good and loving Father to provide for our needs in whatever wilderness we may find ourselves, as we look toward Mount Zion and the heavenly Jerusalem.

Take-away Treasure

A song for pilgrims ascending to Jerusalem. A psalm of David.

> *Lord, my heart is not proud;*
> *my eyes are not haughty.*
> *I don't concern myself with matters too great*
> *or too awesome for me to grasp.*
> *Instead, I have calmed and quieted myself,*
> *like a weaned child who no longer cries for its*
> *mother's milk.*
> *Yes, like a weaned child is my soul within me.*
> *O Israel, put your hope in the LORD—*
> *now and always. (Psalm 131)*

CHAPTER 2

"He Lets Me Rest in Green Meadows"

The Good Shepherd

The LORD is my shepherd;
    I have all that I need.
He lets me rest in green meadows;
    he leads me beside peaceful streams.
He renews my strength.

PSALM 23:1-3

For this week's study, read Psalm 23 and Mark 6.

If anyone had an overly busy schedule, it was Jesus during his years of ministry on this earth. Wherever he went, the crowds gathered, the sick needed healing, and the people were starved for spiritual nourishment. There were occasions when he and the disciples didn't even have time to eat. One of these times is recorded in Mark 6. The Twelve had just returned from being sent out by Jesus, and after they had given him their reports, he said, "Let's go off by ourselves to a quiet place and rest awhile" (v. 31).

But we need to set the stage first to understand why Jesus said this (besides the fact that they just really needed a break). Right before this scene, Mark writes in detail about John the Baptist's imprisonment by Herod Antipas. After pleasing the king with her dancing, Herodias's daughter asked Herod for John's head on a tray, which is what happened. John's disciples came and took away his body for burial. Matthew 14:13–14 describes Jesus' reaction to John's death:

> *As soon as Jesus heard the news, he left in a boat to a remote area to be alone. But the crowds heard where he was headed and followed on foot from many towns. Jesus saw the huge crowd as he stepped from the boat, and he had compassion on them and healed their sick.*

Jesus needed some peace and quiet, and so did the disciples after their ministry journey. Undoubtedly, he grieved at John's death, and he was weary from constantly being with people and helping them (and also dealing with their amazing unbelief in light of so many miracles). He was God in human flesh, but he was still human flesh. He truly needed some breathing room. Yet he didn't roll his eyes and grumble when he saw the crowd of people awaiting him on the shore in what he had hoped would be a "quiet place." No, Scripture says that "he had compassion on them and healed their sick."

As tired and sad as he may have been, he proceeded to lay out a feast for them all. Apparently this "quiet place" was also quite remote, and the disciples were concerned that it was getting late and the people didn't have any food. When

Jesus asked the disciples how much food they had, they reported, "Five loaves of bread and two fish."

> *Then Jesus told the disciples to have the people sit down in groups on the green grass. So they sat down in groups of fifty or a hundred. Jesus took the five loaves and two fish, looked up toward heaven, and blessed them. Then, breaking the loaves into pieces, he kept giving the bread to the disciples so they could distribute it to the people. He also divided the fish for everyone to share. They all ate as much as they wanted, and afterward, the disciples picked up twelve baskets of left-over bread and fish. A total of 5,000 men and their families were fed from those loaves! (Mark 6:39–44)*

The image of Jesus having them sit down "on the green grass" should make us immediately think of that other famous green grass: "He lets me rest in *green* meadows" (Psalm 23:2). In the King James Version, it is more of an imperative: "He *maketh* me to lie down in green pastures."

Jesus is the Good Shepherd of Psalm 23. He not only has us sit down on the green grass (and in ancient cultures, they would have eaten while lying down more than sitting up, hence "rest" or "lie down"), but he also prepares a feast before us in the presence of our enemies. Our cup therefore "overflows with blessings," and we know that his "goodness and unfailing love" will "pursue" us "all the days" of our lives, and that we "will live in house of the LORD forever."

This is something we can take to heart today, whatever our situation. We all need healing and we all need the bread of life. The people of Jesus' day felt this as well, but they didn't understand him at the time or what he was doing. Even the disciples didn't fully understand until after Jesus' resurrection and ascension and the arrival of the Holy Spirit.

With Jesus, miracle followed miracle. When it grew dark and he hadn't yet returned to the Twelve, they became antsy and decided to head back over the Sea of Galilee toward Capernaum. When they were a few miles out, the wind picked up and the water started getting rough, and then they saw Jesus walking on the water toward them. John says that "they were terrified, but [Jesus] called out to them, 'Don't be afraid. I am here!'" (John 6:19–20).

> *I will not be afraid,*
> *for you are close beside me.*
> *Your rod and your staff*
> *protect and comfort me. (Ps. 23:4)*

The next day, the crowd he had just fed came looking for another free meal. Jesus knew this was why they wanted to be with him, that they didn't understand the *meaning* of the miracle of feeding so many people with so little. After they argued about how Moses gave their ancestors bread from heaven, Jesus announced that *he* was the bread from heaven and reminded them that it was *God* who fed the Israelites during their time in the wilderness. Jesus is the "bread of life. Whoever comes to me will never be hungry again" (John 6:35).

Let us look to the Good Shepherd who feeds us, who gives us rest, who renews our strength (restores our souls), who guides us, who heals us and comforts us. Let us lie down on the green grass (perhaps even literally!) and partake in the feast he spreads before us, believing in *him,* the One whom God has sent.

Suffer us not to mock ourselves with falsehood
Teach us to care and not to care
Teach us to sit still
Even among these rocks,
Our peace in His will
—*T. S. Eliot, "Ash Wednesday"*

As you study this chapter, take a minute to close your eyes, breathe in deeply, and think of softly flowing streams and grassy riverbanks. "Let the peace that comes from Christ rule in your hearts" (Colossians 3:15).

1. Read John 10. How is Jesus the "Good Shepherd"? Who are his "sheep" and how do they "know his voice"? How can we today "know his voice"?

2. What is the connection between this New Testament image of the Good Shepherd and the one in Psalm 23? Read Psalm 23 again along with John 10, thinking of Jesus as your shepherd. How does Psalm 23 apply to your own life?

3. Why are the people divided over what Jesus says in John 10? As a result, what do those who fail to recognize his "voice" try to do? What about the others who do recognize it?

4. In "A God-Paced Life" (*Everyday Matters Bible for Women*), Cynthia Heald writes that "our lives are often jam packed with responsibilities, commitments, relationships, and ministries. Yet is a busy, hectic, overscheduled, and underrested life really what God has in mind for us?" Does this apply to your life? If so, what can you do to slow down?

5. In *New Seeds of Contemplation*, Thomas Merton says that too many people "cannot believe that they are pleasing God unless they are busy with a dozen jobs at the same time." Are you one of those, especially when it comes to "ministry"? If so, reconsider your life and seek God's direction. If you find you're overdoing it, pray about what you can cut out or delegate to someone else.

6. "He *lets* me rest in green meadows . . ." In case you needed an excuse, this verse is proof that God gives you permission to take a break! What do you need to do to find the rest that Jesus offers, perhaps even on a daily basis? Where can you go for peace and solitude, especially on the most hectic of days? Do you allow yourself (as God intends) one Sabbath day of rest per week? If not, what can you do to mark off this special and necessary time?

If you want to live a spiritual life you must unify your life. A life is either spiritual or not spiritual at all. No [one] can serve two masters.—Thomas Merton

Points to Ponder

Jesus says, "I tell you the truth, I am the gate for the sheep" (read John 10:7–10).

- How is Jesus the "gate" for you? What do you think this means?

- Who are the "thieves and robbers" that came before Jesus?

- What do you think Jesus meant by "a rich and satisfying life"?

Prayer

Lord, teach me to know when to care and when not to care, to sit still, even among these rocks—whatever these rocks may be. Let your peace rule in my heart as I quiet my soul and calm my restless, anxious thoughts. Lead me to those peaceful streams and let me rest, luxuriating in your presence. May I be quiet enough to hear and know your voice, the Good Shepherd of us all.

Add your prayer in your own words.

Amen.

Put It into Practice

"Psalm 23 paints a picture of what a God-paced life can be like. When the Lord is our Shepherd, we have everything we need, so we don't have to worry. In that psalm God tells me to 'rest in green meadows' and that he 'leads me beside peaceful streams' and 'renews my strength.' Leading a God-paced life means allowing the Lord to be our guide so that we can go on the right paths that honor his name."

—Cynthia Heald, "A God-Paced Life," *Everyday Matters Bible for Women*

Take-away Treasure

So deep walls of this world fall
And heaven like light comes pouring in
Sink from your shallows, O my soul
Into eternity like springs
We touch the rays of light we cannot see
And feel this light that seems to sing
Praises and canticles anticipate each day
The bells to greet the dawn

—John Michael Talbot, "The Woodlands/Praises and Canticles" (adapted from Thomas Merton), *Meditations from Solitude*

CHAPTER 3

"Rivers of Living Water"

God Calling

"Is anyone thirsty?
  Come and drink. . . .
Come to me with your ears wide open.
  Listen, and you will find life. . . ."
Seek the LORD while you can find him.
  Call on him now while he is near. . . .
"My thoughts are nothing like your
    thoughts," says the LORD.
  "And my ways are far beyond anything
    you could imagine."

ISAIAH 55:1, 3, 6, 8

For this week's study, read Isaiah 55 and John 7:37–39.

God's thoughts are nothing like our thoughts and his ways are far beyond our ways. All our understanding is nothing unless God breathes life into us, enlightening the eyes of our hearts (as Paul says in Ephesians 1:18). This is why it is so critical to get away from our everyday life and be quiet before him, listening to him, learning from him.

In "Time Alone versus Engagement with the World" (*Everyday Matters Bible for Women*), Richard Foster writes:

> *Solitude teaches us to live in the presence of God so that we can be with people in a way that helps them rather than manipulates them. Solitude also teaches us how to love God's ways; in time alone we learn the cosmic patience of God. . . . [Isaiah 55 describes] how God's mysterious ways are like the rain that comes down and waters the earth. It descends and disappears, and then up comes life. It's that type of patience.*

Patience is a virtue that increases in us as we practice it—something not easy in our manic society today. But think about how patient God is with us, waiting for us to listen to his voice and heed his call. It is interesting to note that *patience* comes from the Greek word for *suffering*. When we are patient (according to the official dictionary definition), we calmly bear pains or trials without complaint; we are not hasty or impetuous but steadfast despite opposition, difficulty, or adversity. But how can we even begin to attempt this seemly heroic feat without God's strength or wisdom? And how can we have that strength or wisdom unless we spend time with him, praying, studying the Scriptures—and most importantly of all, *listening*?

On the last day, the climax, of the Festival of Tabernacles or Shelters (Sukkot)—a joyous celebration of the autumn harvest of grapes and olives, commemorating God's provision for his children—Jesus reminded Israel that God was still calling. John writes: "Jesus stood up and shouted to the crowds, 'Anyone who is thirsty may come to me! Anyone who believes in me may come and drink!' " (John 7:38).

Scholars suggest that whenever Jesus quoted the first line of an Old Testament passage, he wanted his hearers to think back to the entire passage. He did this on the cross when he called out, "My God, my God, why have you abandoned me?" alluding clearly to Psalm 22. Although it starts with that question seemingly of despair, verse 24 says: "He has *not* ignored or belittled the suffering of the needy. He has *not* turned his back on them, but has listened to their cries for help" (emphasis added). Likewise, God did *not* abandon Jesus on the cross. He heard his cry. Death and sin were destroyed, the power of the strongman (Satan) was broken, and Jesus was victorious.

So when Jesus cried out *"Anyone who is thirsty may come to me!"* he was referring back to Isaiah 55: *"Is anyone thirsty? Come and drink."* But what exactly is this offered water? For all those who come to Jesus and drink, "The Scriptures declare, 'Rivers of living water will flow from his heart'" (John 7:38). In a parenthetical aside in verse 39, John writes: "(When he said 'living water,' he was speaking of the Spirit, who would be given to everyone believing in him.)" The Father longs to give the Holy Spirit to anyone who asks, just as he seeks those who will worship him in spirit and in truth.

> *"My thoughts are nothing like your thoughts,"*
>   *says the* LORD.
> *"And my ways are far beyond anything you*
>   *could imagine."*

Truly, in God coming down to us in human form, living among us, feeding us, teaching us, even shouting to us, we know indeed that his ways are far beyond anything we could ever imagine!

"I am *the bread of life.* Whoever comes to me will never be hungry again. Whoever believes in me will never be thirsty." *(John 6:35; emphasis added)*

"But the time is coming—indeed it's here now—
when true worshipers will worship the Father in
spirit and in truth. The Father is looking for those
who will worship him that way." *(John 4:23)*

*As you study this chapter, think about your daily need
for bread and water, not only physically but spiritually.
Do you nourish your soul as you do your body?*

1. Why do you think Jesus waited until the last and greatest day of the festival to say what he said? And why do you think he shouted (or as other translations say, spoke in a loud voice)? What is the significance of this particular festival in light of what Jesus says?

2. Read the story of Jesus and the Samaritan woman at the well in John 4:4–42. What stands out the most to you? According to some traditions, she is known as Photini, which means "light bearer." How does this tie in to the passage?

3. In John 7:39, John says that this "living water" is the Holy Spirit. Write down what you think about Jesus' statement to the woman: "Those who drink the water I give will never be thirsty again. It becomes a fresh, bubbling spring within them, giving them eternal life." How is the Holy Spirit a "fresh, bubbling spring" within those who believe? How can we "drink the water" Jesus gives?

4. In "The Samaritan Woman: Inviting Others to Reconcile with God" (*Everyday Matters Bible for Women*), Frederica Mathewes-Green says that this woman's reputation probably made her unpopular in certain circles. But after meeting Jesus, she returned to her village, crying out, "Come and see a man who told me everything I ever did!" Mathewes-Green writes, "Her unsavory past, the cause of that estrangement, is now the first thing she brings up. Her brokenness has become her bold witness!" Why do you think she was suddenly so bold?

5. Read again Isaiah 55:8 and compare it with Proverbs 3:5–8. How can you remind yourself that God's ways are far above your ways and not to lean on your own understanding? How can you "seek his will in all that you do"?

6. Proverbs 3:7 says to "fear the LORD and turn away from evil. Then you will have healing for your body and strength for your bones." What do you think it means to "fear the LORD"? Why does Scripture talk about physical healing and strength in connection with this?

As the deer longs for streams of water,
so I long for you, O God.
I thirst for God, the living God.
When can I go and stand before him?
(Psalm 42:1–2)

Points to Ponder

In *New Seeds of Contemplation*, Thomas Merton writes, "In spite of all your misgivings you realize that you are going somewhere and that your journey is guided and directed and that you can feel safe."

+ Do you think the woman at the well felt that way after she spoke with Jesus?

+ Do you feel you are "going somewhere" in your own life? If not, why not?

+ How can you know that God is guiding and directing your journey? Do you feel "safe"?

Prayer

Father, help me to be a true worshiper who worships you in spirit and in truth. Let me drink from the living water you give through the Holy Spirit, and help me to trust in you with all my heart, always remembering that your ways are indeed higher than my ways.

Add your prayer in your own words.

Amen.

Put It into Practice

"When there is no time to do it, that's when you most need to unclutter the calendar and go apart to pray. When the gridlock in your schedule relentlessly forbids it is the time you most need to retreat. That is when your heart beats against the prison walls of your enslavement and says, 'Yes, Lord, I want to spend time with you.'"
—Emilie Griffin, *Wilderness Time*

Take-away Treasure

"Over the years I have learned that my greatest need as a human being is to experience God's unconditional love and presence beyond all that I do for him. I need to hear a voice that is not my own speaking those things that I most need to hear. In the regular practice of solitude, God's unconditional love and presence become the bedrock of my being, the unshakeable foundation of my true identity and calling."

—Ruth Haley Barton, "Leading through Solitude," *Everyday Matters Bible for Women*

CHAPTER 4

"Surely the LORD Is in This Place"

Wrestling with God

"I will not let you go unless you bless me."

GENESIS 32:26

For this week's study, read Genesis 28 and 32 and John 2.

One of the main points of solitude is coming before God in all honesty, searching your soul, seeking your *true* self—that is, who you are in Christ. But sometimes this is painful, very painful. You can end up feeling like a recently plowed field. The field has been churned up—all the weeds, everything, pulled up or worked into the soil—made ready for a time of rest, after which new seeds will be planted for new growth, new life.

When we come before God, the only way to be truly honest is to unmask ourselves. All of us wear masks of one sort or another—sometimes intentional, sometimes not—as we hide behind whatever persona we wish for others to see. It is not easy to take away these masks. As Ruth Haley Barton writes in *Invitation to Solitude and Silence*:

> *We're not sure there is any other self than the self we have constructed in reaction to the wounds and pains of our life. We have identified with this adapted self for so long and so relied on its energy to propel us forward that we don't know who we will be if this self dies.*

We can carry so much pain, hurt, and anger within us that we're afraid to let it go. We've carried it for so long that we feel we would be empty without it, less ourselves. It is true, however, that if we confess this pain and give it up to the Lord, we will indeed have an empty place where it had festered. But the answer to this is to allow *Jesus* to fill up that place with his love, grace, and compassion.

But still, like David in Psalm 55:6–7, we cry out:

> *Oh, that I had wings like a dove;*
> *then I would fly away and rest!*
> *I would fly far away*
> *to the quiet of the wilderness.*

While David was longing to escape his very real enemies, we think that if we could just get away to . . . (fill in your location of choice), then everything would be all right. But if the enemy we're trying to run from is ourselves, then we need to realize sooner rather than later that wherever we go, we take ourselves with us!

In the book of Genesis, Jacob seemed to be on the run quite a bit—mostly from his brother Esau, but also from himself. When he fled to the wilderness, he confronted not only his scheming self but also God. In Genesis 28:11, Jacob found a "good place to set up camp" and stopped for the night. Finding for a pillow a rock "as hard as his head" (as songwriter Michael Card puts it), he had a most remarkable dream.

> As he slept, he dreamed of a stairway that reached from the earth up to heaven. And he saw the angels of God going up and down the stairway. At the top of the stairway stood the Lord, and he said, "I am the Lord, the God of your grandfather Abraham, and the God of your father, Isaac. . . . One day I will bring you back to this land. I will not leave you until I have finished giving you everything I have promised you." (Genesis 28:12–15)

When Jacob awoke from the dream, he declared: "Surely the Lord is in this place, and I wasn't even aware of it!" (28:16). He realized that this was "none other than the house of God, the very gateway to heaven!" (28:17). The next morning, he took his stone pillow and set it up as a memorial pillar, calling the place "Bethel," which means "house of God."

Years passed and Jacob found himself once again alone in his camp. Esau was coming to meet him with four hundred men, and Jacob feared for his life, as well as the lives of those traveling with him. Desperate, he prayed to the God he had met back in Bethel, reminding God of his promise and now asking for protection from Esau.

Genesis 32:24 says that "a man came and wrestled with him until the dawn began to break." When the man could not overpower Jacob, "he touched Jacob's hip and wrenched it out of its socket" (32:25). Apparently recognizing his opponent, Jacob refused to release his hold: "I will not let you go unless you bless me" (32:26). The result was that Jacob received the new name of "Israel" because he had "fought with God and with men and . . . won" (32:28). (*Yisra'el* could mean "God fights" or "God rules.")

When Jesus was in the process of gathering his twelve apostles, he said to Nathanael, "I tell you the truth, you will all see heaven open and the angels of God going up and down on the Son of Man, the one who is the stairway between heaven and earth" (John 1:51).

Jesus is the stairway to heaven that Jacob had seen in his dream. Jesus is the one we meet in the wilderness, the one with whom we wrestle, the one from whom we receive a "stone . . . engraved [with] a new name that no one understands except the one who receives it" (Revelation 2:17). So let us remove our masks and look to him with honesty, not wishing to flee to the wilderness to escape, but holding on to him for dear life as he blesses us.

[Going] from a false sense of self to painful self-recognition . . . is the only place where listening to God can happen.—Columba Stewart

As you study this chapter, think about what you may be struggling with right now and how God can bless you through it or even despite it.

1. "Busyness, noisiness, crowdedness—all of these help us avoid inner struggles, tuck away hidden pain, turn down the volume on inner cries," writes Carla Barnhill in "Dark Solitude" (*Everyday Matters Bible for Women*). What are you avoiding? What "inner cries" are you trying to ignore?

2. Do you find it painful to sequester yourself from other people? Do you try to fill your life up so you don't have to stop to think about what you're really feeling?

3. Barnhill writes, "Jesus, who also experienced anguish in solitude, is with you, even as you feel 'crushed with grief'" (read Mark 14:32–42). Can you sense Jesus with you in the hard times, when you're just barely holding on? If not, why not?

4. Read Romans 8:26. Have you had times when you didn't know how to pray or what exactly to pray for, when all you could do was groan? Did you feel God heard your wordless cry?

5. Read Romans 8:27. Does it help you to know that Spirit actually pleads for you, and that he does this "in harmony with God's own will"? Does this bring you comfort? If so, how?

6. Read Romans 8:28. Why do you think this is one of the most-quoted verses in all of Scripture? Now read Romans 8:18–30 and write down some thoughts that come to you.

Go into your room, shut your door, and call upon Jesus, your Beloved. Stay with him in the privacy of your own room, for you will not find such peace anywhere else. —*Thomas à Kempis*

Points to Ponder

In his book *Monk Habits for Everyday People: Benedictine Spirituality for Protestants*, Dennis Okholm writes about a time at Blue Cloud Abbey when he was walking with one of the brothers: "For a reason I cannot remember he wagged his finger at me and said, 'You like to be in control, don't you?' Translation: 'You are not humble.' Humility breaks down our egoistic fantasies and our need to be in control—our need to be the exception. . . . Humility requires what Columba Stewart calls 'radical self-honesty.'"

- Do you feel that you always need to be in control?

- What is not humble about wanting to be in control?

- How would you define "radical self-honesty"?

Prayer

Lord, help me to come before you as I truly am: without any masks, without any excuses, humble, open, and vulnerable. Help me to look at myself with "radical self-honesty," always remembering how much you love me. I give you whatever pain is lodged deep in my heart. May I find myself completely in you.

Add your prayer in your own words.

Amen.

Put It into Practice

"Thoreau put it well. As our inward quiet life fails, 'we go more constantly and desperately to the post office,' but 'the poor fellow who walks away with the greatest number of letters, proud of his extensive correspondence, has not heard from himself this long while. . . . Read not The Times,' he concludes, 'read the Eternities!' "

—Dallas Willard, *The Spirit of the Disciplines*

Take-away Treasure

"Humility contains in itself the answer to all the great problems of the life of the soul. . . . Humility is the surest sign of strength."

—Thomas Merton, *New Seeds of Contemplation*

Notes / Prayer Requests

Notes / Prayer Requests

Contemplation

CHAPTER 1

"If You Give Up Your Life"

The Way of the Cross

"If you refuse to take up your cross and follow me,
you are not worthy of being mine.
If you cling to your life, you will lose it;
but if you give up your life for me, you will find it."

MATTHEW 10:38-39

For this week's study, read Matthew 27:11–44.

Reading Jesus' words from Matthew 10:38–39 can shock us and even dismay us. How can he possibly expect us to "take up" our "cross" and follow him? What does this mean?

Crucifixion (from which the word *excruciating* derives) was a notoriously slow, agonizing process of capital punishment. Not only was it painful, but it was also humiliating and meant to deter others from a similar horrific fate. In ancient Rome, crucifixion was usually reserved for the lower classes or slaves—or insurrectionists. Cicero called it "a most cruel and disgusting punishment."

Before being nailed (or tied) to it, the condemned person was forced to carry the crossbeam—which could weigh as much as a hundred pounds—to the place of the execution. We see this clearly in the Gospel accounts when Jesus bore on his flogged back that heavy beam of solid wood, dragging himself under the weight of it, until the Roman soldiers forced Simon of Cyrene to carry it for a while.

We know about that fateful Friday in ancient Roman-occupied Palestine and the suffering that Jesus endured on our behalf, but what does he mean by *us* taking up *our* cross and following him? How does this relate to us over two thousand years later?

In Luke 9:21–24, Jesus told his disciples that he would "suffer many terrible things." He would be rejected and killed and then raised from the dead on the third day. He turned to the crowd and said, "If any of you wants to be my follower, you must turn from your *selfish ways*, take up your *cross daily*, and *follow me*. If you try to hang on to your life, you will lose it. But if you give up your life for my sake, you will save it."

Jesus wants us to turn from our "selfish ways," which means that first we need to identify what these may be. This is one of the hardest and yet most beautiful aspects of the contemplative life—turning away from ourselves and seeking only the kingdom of God. He also calls us to take up our "cross daily." This means we need to seek after the ways of the Lord—Monday through Friday, Saturday and Sunday—dying daily to our old ways, ever moving forward to authentic life. When we do these things, we can then "follow" him and be his disciples, worthy to be called "his."

Lest we fear going that far, we must remember that without him we are already dead—dead in our sins and long-time captives of the Enemy of humanity. But here is the good news as presented by the Apostle Paul in Colossians 2:13–15:

> *Then God made you alive with Christ, for he forgave all our sins. He canceled the record of the charges against us and took it away by nailing it to the cross. In this way, he disarmed the spiritual rulers and authorities. He shamed them publicly by his victory over them on the cross.*

An instrument of torture and agonizing death became a means of disarming the "spiritual rulers and authorities." What was meant to humiliate the victim became a way of shaming the victimizer. But in this, we don't mean the Roman Empire against a typical insurrectionist. This was victory on a *cosmic* scale as Jesus disarmed Satan—the original Rebel—and humiliated *him* at the cross. Just when Satan thought he was victorious, Jesus destroyed Death and Sin, and Satan's power over this world and us was forever destroyed.

> *Then Jesus shouted out again, and he released his spirit. At that moment, the curtain in the sanctuary of the Temple was torn in two, from top to bottom. The earth shook, rocks split apart, and tombs opened. The bodies of many godly men and women who had died were raised from the dead. They left the cemetery after Jesus' resurrection, went into the holy city of Jerusalem, and appeared to many people.*

> *The Roman officer and the other soldiers at the crucifixion were terrified by the earthquake and all that happened. They said, "This man truly was the Son of God!" (Matthew 27:50–54)*

Even before his victory on the cross, every time Jesus cast out a demon (or demons in the case of "Legion"), he revealed his power over the Enemy. In Luke 11:14–26, when the crowd around him absurdly accused him of working with Satan in order to have power over demons, he responded:

> *"Any kingdom divided by civil war is doomed. A family splintered by feuding will fall apart. . . . But if I am casting out demons by the power of God, then the Kingdom of God has arrived among you. For when a strong man like Satan is fully armed and guards his palace, his possessions are safe—until someone even stronger attacks and overpowers him, strips him of his weapons, and carries off his belongings. Anyone who isn't with me opposes me, and anyone who isn't working with me is actually working against me."*

In Jesus, we have life, everlasting life. So what really is there left to lose? Keeping this in mind—that victory and life have already been achieved—we gladly turn from our own misguided and confused ways to follow after him. He does not give us more than we can bear, and we do not carry our crosses alone. He is there to help with the burden. Remember his words from Matthew 11:28–30: "Come to me, all of you who are weary and carry heavy burdens. Take my yoke upon you. Let me teach you, because I am gentle and humble at heart, and you will find rest for your souls. For my yoke is easy to bear, and the burden I give you is light." Let them encourage you to truly follow after him, as he simultaneously goes before and beside you.

He himself is my contemplation; he is my delight. Him for his own sake I seek above me.—Isaac of Stella

As you study this chapter, think about what it means for you to pick up your cross, die to yourself, and follow after Jesus.

1. Read Luke 11:24–26. Why do you think that when "an evil spirit leaves a person, it goes into the desert, searching for rest"?

2. Compare the above passage with Jesus' testing in the wilderness in Luke 4:1–13. Why do you think the desert seems to be a dwelling place for evil spirits?

3. What in your life tends to come between you and God, and what can you do about it? What needs to change on your part?

4. Thomas Merton says that "despair is the absolute extreme of self-love." What do you think that means? Can you see any such "despair" in your own life?

5. What does it mean to "give up your life"? Have you ever made any major sacrifices out of love for someone else? Has anyone ever done this for you?

6. Aware of the spiritual battle that rages around us, Paul calls us to be "children of God, shining like bright lights" (Philippians 2:15). What does this mean for your own life? Do you live in the reality of the in-breaking kingdom of God, where the Foe is already vanquished and Christ is the victor? If not, what can you do to remind yourself daily of this truth?

Because of the joy awaiting him, he endured the cross, disregarding its shame. Now he is seated in the place of honor beside God's throne. (Hebrews 12:2)

Points to Ponder

Here are some gems from *New Seeds of Contemplation* by Thomas Merton. How do these apply to your life of contemplation?

- "The beginning of contemplation is faith."

- "True faith must be able to go on when everything else is taken away from us."

- "When it comes to times of darkness . . . then we find out whether or not we live by faith."

- "As long as there is an 'I' that is the definite subject of a contemplative experience . . . then we have not yet 'gone out of Egypt.'"

Prayer

Lord, show me how to pick up my cross daily and follow after you. Let my thoughts be your thoughts, my actions your actions, my love your love, my will your will. May my eyes be so completely focused on you that I forget all about myself. Help me always to live by faith in these days of the already and the not yet.

Add your prayer in your own words.

Amen.

Put It into Practice

"This is what it means to bear one's cross: it means not saying, 'It's my life, entirely at my disposal; I can do with it whatever I want; I have a right to take for myself whatever I can get.' Instead it means to say, 'My life is in God's hands. My life is hidden with Christ in God. I am called to be as much like Christ as I can be, right here in the midst of evil and in spite of the suffering it may bring me.'"
—Lena Malmgren, *Barbed Wire and Thorns*

Take-away Treasure

"Let all our employment be to know God; the more one knows Him, the more one desires to know Him. And as knowledge is commonly the measure of love, the deeper and more extensive our knowledge shall be, the greater will be our love; and if our love of God were great, we should love Him equally in pains and pleasures."

—Brother Lawrence, *The Practice of the Presence of God*

CHAPTER 2

"Blessed Are the Pure in Heart"

Living as Children of God

> "The people who sat in darkness
> have seen a great light.
> And for those who lived in the land
> where death casts its shadow,
> a light has shined."
>
> From then on Jesus began to preach, "Repent of your sins and turn to God, for the Kingdom of Heaven is near."
>
> MATTHEW 4:16-17

For this week's study, read Matthew 6.

Like the prophets of old and the desert mothers and fathers of the early church, we too journey in our wilderness, out into a proverbial wasteland to seek and wrestle with ourselves and with God. We may not be literally fasting for forty days and forty nights, like Moses or Jesus, but we are truly spiritually famished out there in the parched desert. As poet T. S. Eliot writes in *The Waste Land*:

What are the roots that clutch, what branches grow
Out of this stony rubbish? Son of man,
You cannot say, or guess, for you know only
A heap of broken images, where the sun beats,
And the dead tree gives no shelter, the cricket no relief,
And the dry stone no sound of water. Only
There is shadow under this red rock,
(Come in under the shadow of this red rock).

We need for God to unleash the River of Living Water into this parched wasteland, to hear what the Thunder says from out of the enveloping cloud, and to let the peace that passes all understanding flood our hearts and minds.

God provided for Israel in their journey across the wilderness, providing water from a rock and the bread of heaven, the bread of angels, as they needed it—their daily bread. After Jesus stood firmly against Satan's temptation of him in the wilderness—succeeding in the arid desert where Adam had failed in the bountiful garden—the "devil went away, and angels came and took care of Jesus" (Matthew 4:11). Likewise, we too enter the wilderness, seeking the way of the cross, denying our worldly selves, and desiring only to please God. When we have uncovered our hidden hearts before him in honest prayer and confession, only then can we begin to look to him for that much-needed spiritual nourishment.

This is what the children of Israel received on that famous hillside where Jesus taught what we call the Beatitudes— literally, a "state of bliss." In Matthew 6:3–10, Jesus counterintuitively described as "blessed" those who are "poor," those who "mourn," who are "humble" (or rather "meek"—that is, possessing an *inner strength*), those who "hunger and thirst for justice," those who are "merciful," whose "hearts are pure," who "work for peace," and those who are "persecuted for doing right." He told the crowd the opposite of what the world told them—especially the Zealots who wished to rid their homeland of Rome and its suffocating iron grip.

In his Sermon on the Mount, Jesus taught a new way: "You have heard . . . But *I* say . . ." In this, he showed his authority as the Second Person of the Trinity, the Son of Man, the Son of God. In Matthew 5:43–48 (emphasis below added), it was the great I AM who told them:

> "You have heard *the law that says, 'Love your neighbor' and hate your enemy. But I say, love your enemies! Pray for those who persecute you! In that way, you will be acting as true children of your Father in heaven."*

When the Pharisees asked Jesus which was the "most important commandment in the law of Moses," he answered, "You must love the LORD your God with all your heart, all your soul, and all your mind. This is the first and greatest commandment. A second is equally important: 'Love your neighbor as yourself.' The entire law and all the demands of the prophets are based on these two commandments" (Matthew 34–40). In this he simplified a complicated system of law as given by God to Moses at Mount Sinai. In 1 John 2:29–3:3, the apostle writes:

> *Since we know that Christ is righteous, we also know that all who do what is right are God's children. See how very much our Father loves us, for he calls us his children, and that is what we are! . . . We will be like him, for we will see him as he really is. And all who have this eager expectation will keep themselves pure, just as he is pure.*

This reflects what Jesus said in his sermon (Matthew 5:8–9):

> *"God blesses those whose hearts are pure,*
>   *for they will see God.*
> *God blesses those who work for peace,*
>   *for they will be called the children of God."*

This is what we seek after—to be pure of heart, to work for peace, for *shalom*, to be called the children of God. John reminds us to love one another because this demonstrates that we are part of God's family, which enables us to be powerful witnesses in this world of his kingdom—a kingdom that began breaking in with Jesus' time on earth as he healed the sick and the debilitated, cast out demons, and raised people from the dead. A kingdom that is breaking in and one day will be here in its full glory. It is the kingdom of beauty and peace for which we all long—and of which we are already citizens and ambassadors.

> *God is love, and all who live in love live in God, and God lives in them. And as we live in God, our love grows more perfect. (1 John 4:16–17)*

Let us live in him, loving him and one another, as our love grows more and more perfect.

Pure and genuine religion in the sight of God the Father means caring for orphans and widows in their distress and refusing to let the world corrupt you. (James 1:27)

> **As you study this chapter, think about how you can love God and love your neighbor in a way that is pleasing to God.**

1. Although he never watched it (they didn't have TVs in his monastery), Thomas Merton says in *New Seeds of Contemplation*, "It would seem that television should be used with extreme care and discrimination by anyone who might hope to take interior life seriously." Are any of the programs you watch or that your family watches detrimental to your spiritual life? How about the *amount* watched?

2. Merton also writes, "Our minds are like crows. They pick up everything that glitters, no matter how uncomfortable our nests get with all that metal in them." What uncomfortable "metal" is in your "nest"? What can you do to rid yourself of these glittery, unspiritual things?

3. In *Invitation to Solitude and Silence*, Ruth Haley Barton writes that "desperation is a really good thing in the spiritual life. Desperation causes us to be open to radical solutions, willing to take all manner of risk in order to find what we are looking for." What are you desperate to find in your life? What are you willing to risk to find it?

4. She also writes, "Once we get a little rest, we start to get our perspective back. Rather than reacting to everything around us, we start to have a sense of what is truly called for in our life." Have you experienced this? If so, how did your perspective change?

5. Fire is a known purifier and Scripture uses this analogy to speak about true faith. What "fire" have you gone through where you felt your faith to be stronger, purer, afterward?

6. Water is another element associated with purity. We need pure water to live (and again, Scripture uses this analogy quite a bit, as we've already seen). When the water in your life is muddy (either due to impurities or too much agitation), what can you do to help restore its purity?

When I walk into my day saying yes to God and to the world God has created, an act as mundane as riding the train to work is transformed into deep and joyous prayer.—Vinita Hampton Wright

Points to Ponder

In *Monk Habit for Everyday People: Benedictine Spirituality for Protestants*, Dennis Okholm writes: "Is the monastic balanced life, which puts possessions and relationships and the life of the soul in proper perspective, less real than our consumptive preoccupation with gadgets, television, celebrities, war, and spirit-numbing work? Who has distorted reality: the monk or the materialist?" Write down below whatever in your life fits Okholm's "materialist" category, and what you should do about it:

- _____

- _____

- _____

- _____

- _____

- _____

- _____

- _____

Prayer

Father, help me to be pure in heart and to have an inner strength, focusing on you as I go through each day. Help me to step back and see how I might be muddying the waters of my own spiritual life. Keep me from those things that keep me from you.

Add your prayer in your own words.

Amen.

Put It into Practice

"Elijah and countless spiritual seekers after him have experienced God's presence in solitude and silence as they have pulled back from the noisy, peopled places of their lives. Here we sit our souls down and wait for that which comes from beyond ourselves. Here we give in to desperation and desire until God comes to us and does for us what we cannot do for ourselves."

—Ruth Haley Barton, *Invitation to Solitude and Silence*

Take-away Treasure

"Solitude is the furnace of transformation. . . . [It] is the place of the great struggle and the great encounter—the struggle against the compulsion of the false self, and the encounter with the loving God who offers himself as the substance of the new self."

—Henri Nouwen, *Out of Solitude*

CHAPTER 3

"Stop, Look, and Listen"

Seeking the Beauty of God

> One thing I ask from the LORD,
>   this only do I seek:
> that I may dwell in the house of the LORD
>   all the days of my life,
> to gaze on the beauty of the LORD
>   and to seek him in his temple.

PSALM 27:4 (NIV)

---

*For this week's study, read Psalm 27,
Philippians 2:14–18 and 4:4–20.*

Some reading this study may be thinking that it's all well and good to want to have time in solitude and contemplation, but it's really not practical. We are busy, *too* busy, and we rush from activity to activity, collapsing at the end of the day. Then we rise the next morning and do it all over again. We push ourselves because either we have to or we *feel* we have to. Do we really need to serve on that committee at church *and* work full time *and* help out at the local food pantry *and* be involved in a local community group? Then there's grocery shopping to do, meals to prepare, laundry, housecleaning, and the list goes on and on and on. Where in the world do we find a moment for ourselves, let alone God?

But if we feel too busy to have these times of quiet—even a moment to catch our breath and release the mounting tension—then life is seriously off balance. The spiritual is just as important as the physical. If we go without eating nutritious food, drinking enough fluids, exercising, or resting sufficiently, our bodies will eventually scream in protest. But what about the fragile condition of our hearts, minds, and souls? The more stressed out we get, the more we tend to speak harshly to loved ones or coworkers, drive too fast and become impatient and angry with other drivers, or wish the person in line ahead of us would hurry up. Our shoulders tighten, our stomachs rebel, and our attitudes become downright rotten. Studies have proven that stress is a *killer*. We can't keep it up without serious ramifications to our lives.

So we need solitude and contemplation as much as we need water, food, and sleep. Again, we're not talking about necessarily going off to a retreat (though for the terminally stressed, this may be the only solution!). Even fifteen minutes on a hectic morning, and another fifteen minutes either midafternoon when stress mounts and energy wanes, or in the evening as we wind down for a night's rest. We need to breathe and refocus our thoughts, stepping out of the "fight or flight" response we've been locked into, realizing that we're most likely overacting to quite a bit. It's time to step back—even for five minutes—and survey the day, and ask ourselves if the stress is really worth it. Most likely not.

One way of changing our mind-set is to practice an attitude of gratitude. When we wake in the morning, before we drag ourselves out of bed, we should think about what we're thankful for and commit that day's activities and problems to the Lord. Then at night, before dropping off to sleep, we should rehearse again our many blessings (and they *are* many), thanking God for how he provided for us and led us that day. We need to take time to breathe, really breathe, and feel the tension slip away.

In *Whistling in the Dark*, writer and theologian Frederick Buechner encourages us to slow down, to take time to "stop, look, and listen." There are myriad ways to do this.

> *Literature, painting, music—the most basic lesson that all art teaches us is to* stop, look, *and* listen to life *on this planet, including our own lives, as a vastly richer, deeper, more mysterious business than most of the time it ever occurs to us to suspect as we bumble along from day to day on automatic pilot. In a world that for the most part steers clear of the whole idea of holiness, art is one of the few places left where we can speak to each other of holy things.*

Art helps us "stop, look, and listen" and brings beauty to our lives and, ultimately, a sensibility to what is truly *transcendent*. As contemporary visual artist Chris Anderson says, art helps make "visible the invisible."

In case we think that literature, painting, and music are good in and of themselves, but we don't think Buechner's call to "stop, look, and listen" in this area is important for us, he reminds us that it is also "the most basic lesson that the Judeo-Christian tradition teaches us." After listing examples from the Old Testament prophets, he concludes with Christ:

> *And when Jesus comes along saying that the greatest command of all is to love God and to love our neighbor, he too is asking us to pay attention. If we are to love God, we must first stop, look, and listen for him in what is happening around us and inside us. If we are to love our neighbors, before doing anything else we must see our neighbors. With our imagination as well as our eyes, that is to say like artists, we must see not just their faces but the life behind and within their faces. Here it is love that is the frame we see them in.*

Sometimes we just need to sit quietly in a park, a wooded glen, at the beach or an outdoor café, doing nothing but observing nature and people—*stopping, looking,* and *listening.* We need to surround ourselves with beautiful things—everyday beauty in a flowering plant, soothing music, a favorite poem or inspirational quote. Beauty can be as simple as an arrangement of flowers, a nicely set table, glowing candles, or a gift creatively wrapped. Beauty is also in the embrace of a loved one, laughter from a child, or the aged face of a grandparent. Beauty is all around us, even in the seemingly mundane. But most of all, God himself is Beauty. All we need to do is stop, look, and listen! This is another vital part of the contemplative life—to see the Creator in his creation.

Despite being in prison, Paul wrote a letter to the church in Philippi known as the "joy letter," because joy is a main theme throughout it. "Do everything without complaining and arguing," he writes in 2:14. "Live clean, innocent lives as children of God, shining like bright lights in a world full of crooked and perverse people" (v. 15). He then speaks of joy and even how to achieve *peace*:

*Rejoice in the Lord always. I will say it again: Rejoice! Let
your gentleness be evident to all. The Lord is near. Do not be
anxious about anything, but in every situation, by prayer
and petition, with thanksgiving, present your requests to
God. And the peace of God, which transcends all understanding, will guard your hearts and your minds in Christ Jesus.
(Philippians 4:4–7 NIV)*

Do not be anxious about anything? Sure, Paul, we think to
ourselves, *that sounds great, but you don't know my life! If
you had to deal with everything I have to deal with, you'd
be anxious alright!* But he does know us, just as he knew
the church in Philippi and even his own harried life with its
burdens. If anyone had a right to be anxious, it was Paul. But
Jesus told us not to be anxious. It doesn't do us any good and
only makes things worse. Trust in God. "The Lord is near."
Instead of being stressed out and on edge, we need to let our
"gentleness be evident to all." Calm, cool, collected.

We need to remember that our lives are precious to God. If,
as Jesus said, the Father knows the number of hairs on our
heads, then surely he holds us safely in the palm of his hand.
He knows our needs, he knows our frustrations, and he
therefore calls on us to *trust him*. "The Lord is near." If we
pray and give thanks—practice the discipline of gratitude in
a life of contemplation—then *"the peace of God, which transcends all understanding"* will guard our hearts and minds
in Christ Jesus.

*And now, dear brothers and sisters, one final thing. Fix your
thoughts on what is true, and honorable, and right, and pure,
and lovely, and admirable. Think about things that are excel-
lent and worthy of praise. Keep putting into practice all you*

learned and received from me—everything you heard from me and saw me doing. Then the God of peace will be with you. (Philippians 4:8–9)

———————— ❧ ————————

Learn to listen to the music of your own lengths of time, your own silences.—Frederick Buechner

As you study this chapter, think about the everyday beauty in your life and how often you really notice it.

1. Is your life too hectic? If so, what can you cut out or delegate to others? If someone you love is overwhelmed, what can you do to help them? If nothing else, pray about how you can be a calming influence in their life.

2. Louisa May Alcott writes that "the power of finding beauty in the humblest things makes home happy and life lovely." Look around your home and make a list of everything you find beautiful. If you have children at home, have them do the same exercise.

3. Likewise, French painter Camille Pissarro says, "Blessed are they who see beautiful things in humble places where other people see nothing." In what other "humble places" do you find beauty? Try to be more intentional in seeking out the beauty around you on a daily basis, giving thanks and praise to the Creator for it.

4. Do the arts play any role in your life or in the life of your family? Instead of having the television on during dinner (while eating on the couch!), how about putting on some soothing music and sitting down at a nicely set table, and maybe even light some candles? What are some ways you can take this time to catch up with each other and slow down the day?

5. Instead of plopping in front of the TV at the end of a busy day, try going out for a walk instead, or think of something else that's relaxing. What can you do differently with your evening?

6. What are some ways you can "stop, look, and listen"? What about keeping a journal, writing down your aesthetic experiences as they come to you? (An aesthetic experience, for example, is a sunset that takes your breath away and then leads you to recognize the beauty of our Creator God, resulting in praise and worship.)

For me, every hour is grace. And I feel gratitude in my heart each time I can meet someone and look at his or her smile.—Elie Wiesel

---

Points to Ponder

In *Thoughts in Solitude,* Thomas Merton writes, "In our age everything has to be a 'problem.' Ours is a time of anxiety because we have willed it to be so. Our anxiety is not imposed on us by force from outside. We impose it on our world and upon one another from within ourselves."

- What is making you anxious and why? What can you do to overcome that anxiety?

- Do you do anything to add to the anxiety of another person (your spouse or children or coworkers)? If so, what and why? What is there within you that is causing this?

Prayer

Lord, help me to slow down, see and smell the roses of your creation. Let me find you and praise you in the beauty of my everyday life. Open my eyes to see the splendor of your creation not only in things of the earth, but also in those you have created in your own image. Help me to love them as you love them.

Add your prayer in your own words.

Amen.

Put It into Practice

"Seeking the face of God in everything, everyone, all the time, and his hand in every happening; this is what it means to be contemplative in the heart of the world. Seeing and adoring the presence of Jesus, especially in the lowly appearance of bread, and in the distressing disguise of the poor."

—Mother Teresa, *In the Heart of the World: Thoughts, Stories and Prayers*

Take-away Treasure

"A [person] should hear a little music, read a little poetry, and see a fine picture every day of his life, in order that worldly cares may not obliterate the sense of the beautiful which God has implanted in the human soul."

—Johann Wolfgang von Goethe, *Wilhelm Meister's Apprenticeship*

CHAPTER 4

"Never Stop Praying"

Living in the Reality of God's Presence

You must have the same attitude
that Christ Jesus had.

PHILIPPIANS 2:5

For this week's study, read Psalm 139 and Philippians 2:1–15.

In Psalm 139, David proclaims that God is present everywhere and that God knows us intimately, seeing us every moment of every day.

*You know what I am going to say
    even before I say it, LORD.
You go before me and follow me.
    You place your hand of blessing on my head.
Such knowledge is too wonderful for me,
    too great for me to understand!
I can never escape from your Spirit!
    I can never get away from your presence!
    (vv. 4–7)*

We can *never* get away from his presence. This means that we don't have to go out somewhere to look for God. God is always with us, *wherever* we are. "Every day of my life was recorded in your book. Every moment was laid out before a single day passed" (v. 16). Knowing all this, how does David respond?

> Search me, O God, and know my heart;
>   test me and know my anxious thoughts.
> Point out anything in me that offends you,
>   and lead me along the path of everlasting life.
>   (vv. 23–24)

What else could he do when he knew that God saw and understood him so completely? When his soul was laid bare before the Almighty, how could he not want to be holy before a holy God? If our thoughts and deeds are known by God before we speak or do them, wouldn't this be enough to make us think twice before speaking or acting? But how can we possibly do this? In our fast-paced lives, it's too easy to say or do the wrong thing, especially unintentionally.

In 1 Thessalonians 5:17, Paul gives us the answer: "*Never stop praying.*" In the full passage, he says, "Always be joyful. Never stop praying. Be thankful in all circumstances, for this is God's will for you who belong to Christ Jesus" (vv. 16–18). As in Philippians, Paul admonishes us to be joyful and thankful. There is no room for anxious thoughts.

We might not always be in a particularly good mood, but we can still be joyful—joyful deep in our being, resting secure in God's never-changing and unending love. We might grumble, but we can stop ourselves and reassess, realizing that after all we truly have cause to be "thankful in all circumstances." If we "never stop praying," then we recognize that we are continuously in the presence of God. When we realize that the "Lord is near" (as Paul writes in Philippians 4), we can then release our anxious thoughts and calm our minds and hearts, resting in "the peace that passes all understanding."

In Philippians 2:5, Paul says that we should have the "same attitude that Christ Jesus had"—that is, putting aside ourselves and taking "the humble position of a slave." Jesus' love for the world ultimately took him to the cross. But the story didn't end for Jesus—or us—at Golgotha or Joseph of Arimathea's tomb.

> *God elevated him to the place of highest honor and gave him the name above all other names, that at the name of Jesus every knee should bow, in heaven and on earth and under the earth, and every tongue confess that Jesus Christ is Lord, to the glory of God the Father. (Philippians 2:9–11)*

Brother Lawrence of the Resurrection (1614–1691) was a cook in a French monastery who sensed and rejoiced in God's omnipresent reality and all-encompassing love. In *The Practice of the Presence of God*, he writes:

> *The time of business does not with me differ from the time of prayer; and in the noise and clutter of my kitchen, while several persons are at the same time calling for different things, I possess God in as great tranquility as if I were upon my knees at the Blessed Sacrament.*

In this way, as we examine our conscience and look seriously at our interior life, we achieve an *inner freedom*. Like Brother Lawrence in his busy kitchen, we too can find peace amid the crisis or chaos of the moment—like the calm eye in a hurricane. If we have the "same attitude that Christ Jesus had," then we will be true children of God. We will love him and our neighbor, being grateful and joyful, and—since we know we are constantly in his presence—always praying.

As we end this study, we may ask how we will know when we are really living a contemplative life. In *New Seeds of Contemplation,* Thomas Merton gives us a glimpse:

> *What happens is that the separate entity that is you apparently disappears and nothing seems to be left but a pure freedom indistinguishable from infinite Freedom, love identified with Love. Not two loves, one waiting for the other, striving for the other, seeking for the other, but Love Loving in Freedom. . . .*
>
> *No despair of ours can alter the reality of things, or stain the joy of the cosmic dance which is always there. Indeed, we are in the midst of it, and it is in the midst of us, for it beats in our very blood, whether we want it to or not.*
>
> *Yet the fact remains that we are invited to forget ourselves on purpose, cast our awful solemnity to the winds and join in the general dance.*

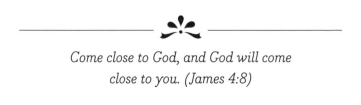

Come close to God, and God will come close to you. (James 4:8)

As you study this chapter, remember that God is present to you at all times and in all places. Be aware of his very real presence as you go about your day.

1. Read James 4:1–10. If you lack peace in your life, ask yourself if there are "quarrels and fights" because you want something for wrong motives. Is there something that may actually be "evil desires at war within you"?

2. Why does James call his readers "adulterers"? What are ways you find yourself being more of a friend "with the world" than with God? What kind of negative consequences have arisen for you from this?

3. Reread Matthew 6:3–12. What does it mean to you to be blessed by God in this way? Which of the Beatitudes is easiest for you to live by? Which is the hardest? Why?

4. Brother Victor-Antoine d'Avila-Latourette is a contemporary monk who cooks and writes just as Brother Lawrence did so many centuries earlier. In *Simply Living the Beatitudes*, he writes, "As we make our small daily efforts to live out these teachings [of the Beatitudes], we experience the sort of inner liberation that Jesus promised to those who followed his way." How can you make "small daily efforts to live out these teachings"? How do you think the Beatitudes can "liberate" you?

5. Brother Victor-Antoine says that in Matthew 6:26–27 "we perceive Jesus teaching to his disciples two very concrete lessons in Gospel living: simplicity and attention to the present moment." How can you make "simplicity and attention to the present moment" real in your own daily life?

6. If Jesus tells us not to worry about our lives, why do we? What can you commit to your heavenly Father right now that you're worried about? Once you've prayed about it, try to forget about it (and then see what happens!).

*We are all invited now, at this very moment, to meet
and encounter God today and listen to his voice.*
—Brother Victor-Antoine d'Avila-Latourette

Points to Ponder

In *Thoughts in Solitude,* Thomas Merton says that we pray "in order that God may hear us and answer us." Read his definition of the "qualities of prayer" below along with the Scriptures provided.

- "Unhesitating faith (Matthew 21:21; James 1:6), which depends on 'singleness' of mind and purpose." What is meant here by "'singleness' of mind and purpose"?

- "Persevering confidence (Luke 11)." What specifically does Luke 11:1–13 say to you about prayer?

Prayer

Father, help me to simplify my life, learning what it means to trust in you to provide for all my needs. Help me also to slow down and live in the moment—moving on from the past and not worrying about the future. Remembering that I am always in your presence, help me to live an authentic life of contemplation.

Add your prayer in your own words.

Amen.

Put It into Practice

"Let all our employment be to *know* God; the more one knows Him, the more one desires to know Him. And as knowledge is commonly the measure of love, the deeper and more extensive our knowledge shall be, the greater will be our love; and if our love of God were great, we should love Him equally in pains and pleasures. . . . Let us seek Him often by faith: He is within us; seek Him not elsewhere."

—Brother Lawrence of the Resurrection, *The Practice of the Presence of God*

Take-away Treasure

A prayer from Brother Victor-Antoine d'Avila Latourette:

> *Lord, our God, You invite us daily*
> *to enter into the mystery of your presence.*
> *You transcend time and space*
> *and dwell in the eternal now.*
> *May your peace, which transcends*
> *all understanding,*
> *keep us rooted in the knowledge and*
> *love of your only Son,*
> *Our Lord Jesus Christ.*

Notes / Prayer Requests

_____

_____

_____

_____

_____

_____

_____

_____

_____

_____

_____

_____

_____

_____

_____

_____

_____

Leader's Guide to

Solitude & Contemplation

It might seem ironic or counterintuitive to be discussing solitude and contemplation in a group setting! But as we see in the study, community is still important. Thomas Merton says, "Do not flee to solitude from community. Find God first in the community, then He will lead you to solitude." And Dietrich Bonhoeffer writes,

> *Let him who cannot be alone beware of community. . . . Let him who is not in community beware of being alone. . . . Each by itself has profound pitfalls and perils. One who wants fellowship without solitude plunges into the void of words and feelings, and one who seeks solitude without fellowship perishes in the abyss of vanity, self-infatuation, and despair.*

Before you start this study, ask each member of your group to share what she thinks "solitude" and "contemplation" mean. After you finish the study, ask again!

Solitude

Chapter 1: Ask your group about the times they have gone on retreat, either with others or as an individual. Ask them about their experience and what they learned or how they grew. If anyone has had what she feels to be a special— maybe even life-changing—encounter with God, ask her to talk about it in detail (if she's comfortable with sharing). Perhaps this would be a good time to arrange a retreat for your group at a place away from the everyday hustle and bustle to practice solitude and contemplation.

Chapter 2: Talk about ways you can find solitude in a hectic life and the importance of finding that much-needed rest. Ask your group members to share how they find time to pull away from their day to recharge themselves. Do they go for a walk, sit on a park bench, or put on soothing music? What are some of their favorite ways to relax and refresh themselves? What about regular quiet times with God?

Chapter 3: Encourage the members of your group to spend time in solitude this week: if they have an office, to shut their door; if they work at home, to find a quiet place away from others. If possible, encourage them to take a day off (or at least half a day) to be by themselves. Encourage them to sit quietly (that is, leave their prayer request list behind!) and *listen for what God has to say to them.*

Chapter 4: If your group is comfortable with this, ask them to confess whatever pain or anger may be festering in them right now, or if there's something (or someone) they're running away from or trying to avoid. As James 5:16 says, "Confess your sins to each other and pray for each other so that you may be healed. The earnest prayer of a righteous person has great power and produces wonderful results." Be honest with one another about any masks you feel you may be hiding behind. Pray for one another for healing, love, and peace.

Contemplation

Chapter 1: Spend time focusing on Jesus—his life, his sacrifice for us, and his victory. Let this be a time of worship and drawing near to the Lord and one another. Perhaps ask members of your group to share their personal testimony of coming to Christ, and what he means in their lives. Talk about how you can live the way of the cross in a busy world. What does this actually mean on a practical, daily basis?

Chapter 2: In reading the Beatitudes, talk about each point Jesus makes and what you think he means by "pure in heart" and so on. What are some ways we can live out the Beatitudes, to be salt and light to those around us? Discuss some practical ways or personal experiences, especially in loving our "enemies" and praying for those who "persecute" us. Do some research on the word *shalom*, and then talk about ways to practice it in your daily lives.

Chapter 3: Discuss the importance of beauty in a person's life, what it means to stop and smell the proverbial (and literal) roses. Ask your group members about specific ways they intentionally create beauty around them and how it affects their lives. Have each group member share something she finds beautiful and why. Encourage the group to "stop, look, and listen" this week, to try and live in each moment, and then report back to the group what they discovered.

Chapter 4: Contemplation is listening in prayer to what God is saying to us, while living in the reality of his presence. Encourage your group to attune their spiritual ears to hearing God's voice, remembering David's words in Psalm 139. By this point, your group should understand that contemplation means living an authentic Christian life, one in which we continuously grow in faith and in love. It is a lifelong process of finding our true selves in God. As Thomas Merton says:

> *Contemplation is the highest expression of [one's] intellectual and spiritual life. It is that life itself, fully awake, fully active, fully aware that it is alive. It is spiritual wonder.* . . . *Contemplation is the awareness and realization, even in some sense* experience, *of what each Christian obscurely believes: "It is now no longer I that live but Christ lives in me."*

For Further Reading

á Kempis, Thomas. *The Imitation of Christ: A New Reading of the 1441 Latin Autograph Manuscript*. Translated by William C. Creasy. Macon, GA: Mercer University Press, 2007.

Anonymous. *The Cloud of Unknowing*. New York: HarperOne, 1981.

Barton, Ruth Haley. *Invitation to Solitude and Silence*. Downers Grove, IL: InterVarsity Press, 2004.

Brother Lawrence. *The Practice of the Presence of God*. Peabody, MA: Hendrickson, 2008.

D'Avila-Latourrette, Brother Victor-Antoine. *Simply Living the Beatitudes*. Ligouri, MO: Ligouri, 2010.

Foster, Richard J., and James Bryan Smith, ed. *Devotional Classics: Selected Readings for Individuals and Groups*. A Renovaré Resource for Spiritual Renewal. New York: HarperCollins, 1989.

Foster, Richard J. *Celebration of Discipline: The Path to Spiritual Growth.* San Francisco: HarperSanFrancisco, 1998.

Merton, Thomas. *Contemplative Prayer.* New York: IMAGE, 1996.

———. *New Seeds of Contemplation.* New York: New Directions, 1972.

———. *Thoughts in Solitude.* New York: Farrar Straus Giroux, 1999.

Norris, Kathleen. *The Cloister Walk.* New York: Riverhead Press, 1997.

Okholm, Dennis. *Monk Habits for Everyday People: Benedictine Spirituality for Protestants.* Grand Rapids: Brazos Press, 2007.

Steindl-Rast, David, and Sharon Lebell. *Music of Silence: A Sacred Journey through the Hours of the Day.* Berkeley: Ulysses Press, 2002.

Willard, Dallas. *The Spirit of the Disciplines: Understanding How God Changes Lives.* San Francisco: HarperSanFrancisco, 1999.